W. H. Auden

by

JAMES D. BROPHY

 Columbia University Press

NEW YORK & LONDON 1970

*R
001
14262*
p. 2

1971

COLUMBIA ESSAYS ON MODERN WRITERS
is a series of critical studies of English, Continental, and other writers
whose works are of contemporary artistic and intellectual significance.

Editor

William York Tindall

Advisory Editors

Jacques Barzun   W. T. H. Jackson   Joseph A. Mazzeo

W. H. Auden is Number 54 of the series

JAMES D. BROPHY
is Professor of English at Iona College.
He is the author of *Edith Sitwell: The Symbolist Order.*

Copyright © 1970 Columbia University Press
ISBN: 0-231-03265-x
Library of Congress Catalog Card Number: 70-126545
Printed in the United States of America

Grateful acknowledgment is made to Random House, Inc.,
and to Faber and Faber Ltd.
for permission to quote from W. H. Auden's poetry.

W. H. Auden

In a century of the symbolist, surreal, and absurd, W. H. Auden is essentially a poet of the reasonable. "Coming out of me living is always thinking," a line from one of his early poems, is perceptive comment indeed by a poet whose difficult passages, while innovative in syntax and diction, usually yield a logical resolution. Although he apologizes for "private joking," obscurity in Auden is minor compared with other important poets of our time, and it is instructive that when he praises the Hermetic spirit as opposed to the Apollonian (in "Under Which Lyre") he does so in absolutely lucid verse. Dissociating himself from what he calls the "Francophile gaggle of pure songsters," Auden practices what Mallarmé never taught.

Wystan Hugh Auden was born in 1907 in York, England, but his family moved to the Midlands the next year when his father, a medical doctor, became the Medical Officer of Birmingham and Professor of Public Health at the university there. Both of Auden's grandfathers were Anglican clergymen; "I was," he tells us, "the son of book-loving, Anglo-Catholic parents." Early in his private schooling Auden showed delight in biology and apparently would have followed in his father's direction if at the age of fifteen, prompted by the question of a friend, he had not suddenly decided to write poetry. His first poem was published in 1924 at the age of seventeen. Although Auden chose to become a poet, his early bent for science is clearly consonant with his abiding interest in logic and the intricate mechanics of prosody.

[3]

After graduating from Oxford (Christ Church), where his first book of poetry was published in his last year (1928), he spent a year in Berlin, the first of an extraordinary number of residencies and travels abroad. From 1930 to 1935 he schoolmastered in England and then went to Iceland with Louis MacNeice in 1936 and to Spain in 1937. And it is from this visit during the Civil War that he dates the beginning of his return to Christianity and the Anglican communion of his parents and grandparents. In Barcelona he writes:

I found as I walked through the city that all the churches were closed and there was not a priest to be seen. To my astonishment this discovery left me profoundly shocked and disturbed. . . . I could not escape acknowledging that however I had consciously ignored and rejected the Church for sixteen years, the existence of churches and what went on in them had all the time been very important to me.

In 1938, the following year, he and Christopher Isherwood traveled to China via the United States, and on their return, in a decision criticized in England, they decided to remain in the States, Auden becoming a citizen in 1946. In America Auden first turned to his former position of schoolmaster and taught for a year at St. Mark's, and thereafter through the early 1950s he took brief appointments at a wide variety of colleges and universities including the New School for Social Research, Bennington, Barnard, and Smith. From 1956 to 1961 he held the elected chair of Professor of Poetry at Oxford. Since the mid-fifties Auden has supported himself by his widely published poetry, lecturing (as distinct from teaching), and reviewing. He now makes his permanent home in an East Greenwich Village apartment (he could afford much better), and having abandoned Italy as a summer residence, in 1957 he purchased a home in Austria where he now spends the spring and summer. Although he is an ardent champion of privacy, his telephone is listed in the Manhattan directory.

[4]

All readers of Auden note a change in his work after 1939, a change some critics interpret as a retreat from the liberal commitment of his poetry in the thirties. The change in style is undeniable—from stressed ellipsis not unlike Hopkins' sprung rhythm to a more relaxed discursiveness. Moreover, Auden himself lends support to the division of his later work from the earlier: since the fifties he has revised and even rejected many of his early and famous pieces like "Petition" and "Spain, 1937" (according to William York Tindall "the best poem of that war"). Nonetheless, an evaluation of his changes and the poetry of his whole career suggests that the Auden who in the sixties has widely praised and translated the young Russian poet Andrei Voznesensky is essentially no less liberal than he was in the thirties, and that the editorial strictures which he now imposes on his own collections (he does not forbid the use of any poem by other editors) are manifestations of an intellectual responsibility which is the basis of the liberality evident in both his periods.

In the Foreword to his recent *Collected Shorter Poems* (1966) Auden states, "Some poems which I wrote and unfortunately, published, I have thrown out because they were dishonest, or bad-mannered, or boring." He further claims that "a dishonest poem is one which expresses, no matter how well, feelings or beliefs which its author never felt or entertained." As example he cites the lines from "Spain, 1937,"

> History to the defeated
> May say Alas but cannot help nor pardon,

which Auden now believes "equate goodness with success," and which he now looks upon "shamefully." Further, according to Auden, "It would have been bad enough if I had ever held this wicked doctrine, but that I should have stated it simply because it sounded to me rhetorically effective is quite inexcusable."

[5]

We learn, therefore, that Auden has omitted "Spain" from his collection, not from a conversion to some reactionary absolutism, but from motives which logically continue his sympathy with the cause of those who fought against absolutism in Spain. For they were eventually the "defeated," and Auden, following the dictate of his "dishonest" lines, would have to withhold from them his "help" and "pardon."

Why Auden rejected "Spain" rather than revise it is not known, but that the lines which he questions are the concluding ones of acknowledged power may be the reason: they may have had an effect that he could not match with honest ones. "Petition," another famous discarded poem, is also dropped because of what he now calls a dishonest statement in the conclusion: ". . . look shining at/ New styles of architecture, a change of heart." Upon reflection, Auden now realizes that he never liked "new styles of architecture." The satiric tone of the poem confirms this analysis and the continuity between "early" and "late" Auden. "Today," Auden recently wrote of his early years, "my notions of what poetry should be are still, in all essentials, what they were then."

In other poems Auden has chosen to edit rather than reject completely. In his long poem "In Memory of W. B. Yeats" he has retained the poem without the three stanzas which pardon cowardice and conceit and which assert that time "will pardon Paul Claudel/ Pardons him for writing well." If anything, the editing of the "late" Auden tends to prove that liberal ideology is still important to him whether successful or not, and that, as in Claudel's case, even a compelling style will not excuse absolutist views.

In 1965, at the age of fifty-eight, Auden wrote that his life so far had been "unusually happy." Stephen Spender, who was two years behind Auden at Oxford, observes in his auto-

[6]

biography the undergraduate manifestation of that happiness. "For his Oxford contemporaries," Spender writes,

the most impressive thing about Auden undoubtedly was that, at such an early age, he was so confident and conscious a master of his situation. . . . At the same time he avoided coming into unnecessary conflict with the interests and views of those around him. As a youth he was outrageous, but he was not a rebel.

The happiness of Auden from an early age and the self-assurance which, according to Spender, made him at Oxford the center of a large circle of friends for whom he was the arbiter of literary taste are consistent with the moderate temperament of his work from the very first collection published (and printed personally) by Stephen Spender at Oxford in 1928. There is nothing of hatred even in his satires, nor in his rational objectivity is there a personal "ax to grind." The most striking attribute of the confident person whom Spender describes is a poetic perception of moderation and magnanimity. Even in the early dramatic poem, "Dance of Death" (1934), which in the depths of the Depression was definitely an anticapitalist work, Auden introduces Marx as a hero at the conclusion of the work with lines from the chorus which are unquestionably satiric of economic absolutism. His liberal political ends have never distorted his liberal vision.

Auden's recognition of complexity in all things is the basis of his analytical moderation and accounts for other important characteristics of his poetry: his humility and defense of the privacy of others, a great interest in the variety of form and genre (especially light verse), and a penchant for verbal surprise.

"I want every poem I write," Auden has written,

to be a hymn in praise of the English language; hence my fascination with certain speech-rhythms which can only occur in an uninflected language rich in monosyllables, my fondness for pe-

[7]

culiar words with no equivalents in other tongues, and my deliberate avoidance of that kind of visual imagery which has no basis in verbal experience and can therefore be translated without loss.

These views particularly accord with his high regard for Voznesensky, of whose poems Auden has made "transliterations." According to Auden, Voznesensky's poems are of genuine talent because they are "untranslatable." Confronting in Voznesensky's startling mixture of irony and nuances of colloquial and traditional diction a poetic sensibility remarkably similar to his own, Auden renders "transliterations" that read like poems of Auden's. (Whether one of the many poets whom Auden has influenced is Voznesensky is an interesting question.)

Auden himself began his practice of using the unusual and "peculiar"—presumably the "untranslatable"—from his very first work. "The Letter," a poem printed in the 1928 volume, is a work which Auden places first in his newly collected edition, and which demonstrates his early—and late—technique of the skillful collocation of the unusual with the traditional. Of course, the achieved effect would not be surprising without the contrast with the formal and the accepted. And this may be a reason why Auden is such a devotee of so many traditional forms such as the ballad, sonnet, ode, and villanelle. Also in his search for what he calls "curious prosodic fauna" he is understandably led to bacchics, choriambs, and alcaics of the classical past which today are both unknown and unused. In this return to the past in literary tradition Auden is not alone among modern poets: Hopkins, for example, to whom Auden is much in debt, found a basis for his curious prosody in Middle and Old English poetry. The search for what is new or what appears new almost always rejects the work of the immediately preceding generation (Auden, for all his praise of Eliot, did

[8]

not continue Eliot's or Pound's style which dominated the twenties), but in so doing frequently returns to language and technique of the more distant past. In his early poem "Something Is Bound to Happen" (1932), later retitled "The Wanderer," Auden's haunting opening line, "Doom is dark and deeper than any sea-dingle," is taken almost exactly from a Middle English homily. The poem in spirit, moreover, is closely analogous to the Old English poem "The Wanderer," which undoubtedly accounts for Auden's new title.

Auden's language in "The Wanderer," aside from being evocatively alliterative, is also redolent of loneliness and typically eccentric in its Anglo-Saxon strangeness (to modern ears):

> . . . lonely on fell as chat
> By pot-holed becks
> A bird stone-haunting, an unquiet bird.

The poem—as with others of Auden's—gains its power by conjoining the remoteness of Anglo-Saxon tone and vocabulary with the modern idiom. The combination is effective: the use of Old English allusively supports the nature of the poem, the synthesis heightens and gives dignity to the modern situation.

In a passage quoted above Auden speaks of his "fascination with certain speech-rhythms which can only occur in an uninflected language rich in monosyllables." One aspect of this interest is especially prominent in the early poetry where the omission of expected monosyllables, particularly the articles necessary to an uninflected language, creates a stressed and anxious tone. The opening stanza of "The Exiles" (1934) is an example of this frequent practice of Auden's:

> What siren zooming is sounding our coming
> Up frozen fjord forging from freedom
> What shepherd's call

> When stranded on hill,
> With broken axle
> On track to exile?

The absence of "the" before "hill" and "track" and the omission of "a" before "broken" suggest the same kind of breathless urgency that similar ellipsis of Hopkins' "sprung rhythm" also creates. The conjunction of "siren" and "zooming" in the opening line is another illustration of Auden's accomplished integration of the old ("siren" evokes the Homeric world) and the new. The contrast is startling, energizing yet organically apposite within the poem that describes the modern predicament with "the gun in the drawer" and in which "our nerves are numb" as "the old wound."

In addition to stating that he seeks a "poetic uniqueness of expression," Auden writes that he aims to combine with that uniqueness the "drab sober truthfulness of prose," one facet obviously setting off—as well as qualifying—the other in the service of variety, the essence of all of Auden's work. "The Letter," the early poem which Auden has now placed first in his newest collection, admirably illustrates the poet's statement. Furthermore, that this earliest of his poems so well conforms to his critical remarks of 1964 supports the view that early and late Auden are not really dichotomous.

"The Letter" earns its initial position with its opening:

> From the very first coming down
> Into a new valley with a frown
> Because of the sun and a lost way,
> You certainly remain.

Here, as well as in the remainder of the short poem (28 lines), we meet the "drab sober truthfulness of prose." There is a "frown" to be adumbrated in the poem by the arrival of the letter which announces that the lover is not to arrive. But the disappointment is not desolation, and the poem seeks to resolve an understanding: in the midst of loss much remains. And, although it is not one of Auden's best poems, the work possesses a "poetic uniqueness of expression" which is balanced with somber, proselike exposition.

There are, for example, several instances of departures from the normal prose order, as in this complex syntactical ellipsis:

> Shall see, shall pass, as we have seen
> The swallow on the tile, spring's green
> Preliminary shiver, passed
> A solitary truck, the last
> Of shunting in the Autumn.

The most successful departure from "drab sober prose," however, is the first of the concluding lines which expresses the poem's resolution:

> I, decent with the seasons, move
> Different. . . .

The tone is reserved but striking. Certainly "decent with the seasons" is not a prose statement; the phrase stands out with the word "decent" anomalous for a pastoral lyric—except one by Auden who indeed moves "different." In context we realize the meaning of "decent" as "fitting" as well as, with the lover's absence, "chaste." Moreover, as the poem moves toward resolution and acceptance, "decent" becomes a pun on "descent," confirming the autumnal mood at the close. Much of Auden's later work down to the present is prefigured here in one of his earliest poems.

Quite obviously, where difficulties occur in Auden's poetry they do not come from his pursuit of the "drab sober truthfulness of prose," but mainly from his desire for "poetic uniqueness of expression." However, even in the prose sections of a long dramatic poem like _Paid on Both Sides_ (1930) one meets the same ellipsis as in the poetry. _Paid_, for example, opens with the remarks "You've only just heard?" and "Dick met me, panted disaster" which introduce us to dramatic speech, the sound of which is especially important. The work is about a tense time of struggle, a kind of anonymous and universal setting of civil war, and immediately we hear the disjointed syntax that is characteristic of Auden's work before 1940. We hear (continuing with the opening of _Paid_): "To Colefangs had to go, would speak with Layard, Jerry and Hunter with him only. They must have stolen news, for Red Shaw waited with ten, so Jerry said, till for last time unconscious. Hunter was killed at first shot. They fought, exhausted ammunition, a brave defence but fight no more."

This breathless cadence, so appropriate to the dramatic situation of this work and many of Auden's poems of this "Age of Anxiety" (a phrase he appears to have later coined in 1947 as the title of a long poem), is difficult only because it is unusual. The ellipsis involved is generally simple and the inversion readily, if not immediately, perceived. Yet the eccentricity is there and, as in "The Wreck of the _Deutschland_," can be, as Bridges remarked about Hopkins' poem, "a dragon folded at the gate to forbid entrance [to the rest of the poetry]."

Of more real difficulty in the realm of syntax is the kind of complexity seen above in the "Shall see, shall pass" sequence of "The Letter," a more famous example of which is the opening of "Petition" (1930), a sonnet which, although one of Auden's most famous and widely quoted poems, is now, as mentioned earlier, dropped from his own official canon. The poem opens with this plea (obviously a parallel of Hopkins' prayer "Thou art indeed just Lord"):

[12]

> Sir, no man's enemy, forgiving all
> But will its negative inversion, be prodigal.

The lines initially present difficulties to the reader, such as the syntax of "will" and the antecedent of "its," and would be easier if Auden had not made the inversion he did, that is, if he had written, ". . . forgiving all/ But its negative inversion will." What justifies the displacement, of course, are two considerations: that Auden always breaks up the "drab sober" prose with "poetic uniqueness," and that this inversion is fitting to this poem about the inversion of modern man, his "distortion of ingrown virginity." The poem seeks reverses:

> Cover in time with beams those in retreat
> That, spotted, they turn through the reverse were great.

And thirdly, with Auden one must realize the possibility of wit which makes an inversion where there is "inversion."

The difficulties of "Petition" when analyzed demonstrate that the order of Auden's complexity is literally within reason and that, although he is not always an easy poet, his difficulties are of a different nature from those of poets like Pound and Eliot who rely on recherché literary knowledge, Dylan Thomas who depends on the irrational, and Yeats who uses private myths. Auden's difficulties are internal and organic and usually are resolved by conventional reasoning—and frequently by a dictionary.

The unusual aspects of Auden which characterize almost every one of his poems are not always, as we have seen already, of a high order of difficulty. And many of them are simple and even conventional. Auden's opening lines, as compelling as Bacon's in prose, frequently incorporate some touch of the "peculiar" such as

> What's in your mind, my love, my coney

from an Auden "Song" of 1933. But he can even give us a sense of the unfamiliar without using a strange word like "coney." Opening lines like " 'O where are you going?' said reader to rider" and " 'We have brought you,' they said, 'a map of the country' " derive their impact from the dramatic cast of the line, although it must be said that the dramatic situations are certainly not commonplace ones for the beginnings of poems. At times the element of the unexpected is irony, which makes Auden very much a poet of his age. In the sonnet "Who's Who" (1933) Auden describes how the "greatest figure of his day" astonished critics by loving a simple, unknown person who ". . . lived at home;/ Did little jobs about the house with skill/ And nothing else." The poem begins:

A shilling life will give you all the facts,

a line which like many others of Auden's is striking without any literal eccentricity. And yet, as Auden says about himself, it is "different." His element of the "peculiar" is often lowkeyed, but it is no less effective for that.

The later poetry of W. H. Auden, that is, his work after 1939, is remarkably similar to the earlier in asserting the unusual. Only in the realm of syntactical distortion is there a change. The later Auden considerably tempers the elliptical tension of his lines that link him so closely with Hopkins and the Old English poets. He becomes more discursive, and like Eliot's transition from the style of *The Waste Land* to the *Four Quartets* there is more philosophy and somewhat less difficulty (although Auden is not so difficult as Eliot in either period).

As with Eliot there is a temptation with Auden to attribute the stylistic change to an increasing religious commitment. Yet this explanation is simplistic and unconvincing. Eliot's

[14]

style in "Ash Wednesday" (1930) did not undergo a change after his confirmation in the Church of England in 1927, and so it is unreasonable to hold the *Quartets*, the first of which appeared eight years later, representative of the conversion. Auden, moreover, did not exclusively employ a style of elliptical stress in his early poetry. "Taller Today" (1928), the famous ode "Which Side Am I Supposed to Be On?" (1932), now retitled simply "Ode," "Dover" (1937), and dozens of other poems, including the widely anthologized "Musée des Beaux Arts" (which Auden now includes in his 1933–38 section), are written in what we recognize as the "later" style. It is difficult to prove, also, that Auden was less happy earlier —if less distress is what caused the later change to a more relaxed tone. For Auden has said in 1965 that he "so far has been unusually happy" without any qualifications about returning to Christianity. And while there are more "light" pieces after 1939, which may argue for relatively more contentment, there is no convincing reason to attribute this new state (if it exists) to his religious commitment. One might as well attribute his change to the new social and political climate which he encountered in the United States: looking back on his departure from England, Auden said, "My instinct to get out was right."

Knowing that Auden's early stressed style was derivative of Hopkins (who could deny the origin of a line like "Would gush, flush, green those mountains and these valleys"?) and realizing that young poets usually outgrow their first masters, one may propose a sound explanation for Auden's change as autonomous, aesthetic growth. And since Auden's late style has a solid grounding in his early period it is demonstrable that the change indeed represents artistic evolution more than ideological conversion.

One of the evident similarities between early and late Auden is the ability to engage the reader at the opening line. "No, Virgil, No" ("Secondary Epic," 1959), "When the Sex War ended with the slaughter of the Grandmothers" ("Song," 1944), "Corns, heartburn, sinus headaches, such minor ailments" ("A Change of Air," 1963) illustrate this continuity of the dramatic. Other opening lines like "He disappeared in the dead of Winter" ("In Memory of W. B. Yeats," 1939) and "Our hill has made its submission" ("Homage to Clio," 1955) show that Auden, as earlier, can compel and appear unique in a subtle way. "In Praise of Limestone" (1948), a poem of long lines and formal dignity, exhibits Auden's abiding love of the unusual word ("Their steep stone gennels") as well as the surprising:

> And not to be pacified by a clever line
> Or a good lay.

And the necessity for contrast and the will to startle extend down through Auden's recent work, as in "Ode to Terminus" (1968):

> . . . that a Thingummy
> so addicted to lethal violence
> should have somehow secreted a placid
>
> tump with exactly the right ingredients
> to start and to cocker Life.

There are, in fact, very few poems of Auden's that do not in some way possess a facet of his disposition to the "peculiar" and "unique." And those poems are the exception that prove the rule—Auden's rule. An Auden poem is one that exploits contrast and the unusual. "If thou must choose," he writes in "Under Which Lyre" (1947), "choose the odd."

One of Auden's friends has said that Auden thinks of himself as a "giant personal enterprise—Auden, Auden, Auden and

Company." The remark is apt, for it suggests that Auden is made up of many Audens, that complexity and variety are the basis of his unique totality. And in no aspect of his work is Auden's multiplicity more evident than in his talent for writing brilliant light or humorous verse concurrently with his serious. No other poet of our century has been able to combine these talents so successfully.

In fact, for a comparable combination of comic and serious talent we may have to go back as far as Byron, whom, not surprisingly, Auden admired and whom he handsomely praised in his "Letter to Lord Byron" (1937). Moreover, both these poets are frequently depreciated for possessing this dual talent; that is, for not being serious enough all the time. Both are somewhat anomalous in their times: Byron in the midst of intensely serious romantics who were at the farthest remove from the comic, Auden surrounded by those dedicated to the heavy burden of setting the wasteland in order. The easiest way for someone to dismiss Auden today is to "honor" him as our finest writer of *light* verse, for as a culture we prefer the dark and weighty. Auden is an astute critic of his times when he observes (in "Letter to Lord Byron"), "Light verse, poor girl, is under a sad weather."

Yet Auden has developed a philosophy of the comic that integrates it with life as it has developed in modern times. "When we consider the history of epic or tragic or lyric art," he writes in "Notes on the Comic" (1952),

we see change but no progress; *Paradise Lost* is different from *The Iliad* but no better. When, however, we consider comic art, it seems to us that the progress has been immense. The jokes in ancient literature seem surprisingly unfunny.

The essential element in the comic, according to Auden, is a sense of individuality in conflict with immutable forces: "A sense of wit and humor develops in a society to the degree that its members are simultaneously conscious of being each a unique individual and of being all in common subjection to unalterable laws." Such a theory perfectly accords with Auden's use of the unique in the context of the familiar. There is sound basis, in fact, for considering Auden, in an appreciative sense, to be essentially a comic poet. Even what appears to be a very serious poem, "Lullaby" (1937), that tender poem of marvelous pathos which begins,

> Lay your sleeping head, my love,
> Human on my faithless arm,

may be considered abstractly as a comic poem. Certainly it is not tragic with its recognition of the

> Mortal, guilty, but to me
> The entirely beautiful,

and its concluding wish that

> Nights of insult let you pass
> Watched by every human love.

The challenge of immutable laws is involved in a tragic situation also, but in the world of tragedy it is always assumed that deviation from those laws, certainly a kind of uniqueness, is wrong. In Auden's work, as well as in his definition of the comic, the uniqueness of the individual is honored, and its clash with the immutable laws of society, therefore, can be something less than tragic, as in "Lullaby," and frequently incontestably comic.

Although much of Auden's poetry, both light and serious, may be basically comic in a philosophical perspective, there is nothing frivolous about his light verse. It is not written, for example, solely for amusement as the appellation "light" generally signifies (especially in disapprobation). Auden, in Robert

[18]

Lowell's estimate, is "constantly writing deeply on the big subjects, and yet keeping something wayward, eccentric, charming, of his own." Part of Auden's approach to the "big subjects" is to write on them in what, in inadequate terminology, we choose to call "light" verse. Lowell finds a "marvelous crackle" in Auden's light verse, and that quality exists because of the special tension which Auden creates in this genre. Just as in a formal ode like "Ode to Terminus" he will incongruously use words like "tump" and "Thingummy" in a kind of comic (and honored) individualism set off against the dominant formality, so in the light verse there are aspects which contrast with or qualify the levity.

The ballad "Miss Gee" (1937) is an example of Auden's light verse which under the alchemy of its "marvelous crackle" becomes something else, transcending what we usually think of as light verse even in such first-rate practitioners as John Betjeman and Ogden Nash. The opening stanza,

> Let me tell you a little story
> About Miss Edith Gee;
> She lived in Clevedon Terrace
> At Number 83,

establishes the traditional ballad tone: rollicking, yet pregnant with disaster. The "little story" of a ballad traditionally is dire although the form belies the misfortunes of the story. There is, in other words, in every ballad something anomalous and ironic, which is perhaps one reason why Auden has used the style so frequently—and so successfully. The form accommodates his sense of contrast and balance, the tension of reality as he understands it.

Auden tells Miss Gee's story in twenty-five stanzas: she is a prim and pious spinster who lives alone knitting for the church bazaar and who dies suddenly of cancer. Consistent with this "little story," the author's attitude is predominantly serious, not for sentimental reasons concerning Miss Gee's unfortunate death, but for the social and moral analysis which Auden reveals in the ballad. Miss Gee prays that she be not led into temptation, that she be made "a good girl, please." As she proceeds to church on a bicycle to which Auden appositely gives a "back-pedal brake" she averts her eyes from the lovers along the path. Yet she has a dream in which the Vicar asks her to dance and chases her through a field as a bull. In further psychological comment the doctor who diagnoses her fatal disease notes that "Cancer's a funny thing,"

> "Childless women get it
> And men when they retire;
> It's as if there had to be some outlet
> For their foiled creative fire."

Clearly the moral of the story is that Miss Gee's death comes from repression, but this is a flaw which Auden chooses to make comic rather than tragic. His sensibility is particularly attuned to the comic, which, as we see in his definition of comedy, is a vision of individuality in conflict with immutable forces that permits a benign estimate of the transgressor. Auden, therefore, brings both sympathy and laughter to Miss Gee. The irony of this dead spinster being "laid" on the table and surrounded by medical students is mordant, but the irony does not exist at all unless we also acknowledge her genuinely pathetic human nature. "Cancer" in the poem indeed is proved to be "a funny thing," but only because it is involved in Auden's complex universe of comic discourse and not in the less compassionate world of tragedy.

"Victor," a companion piece to "Miss Gee" (it appeared in the same issue of *New Verse*), tells a more conventional ballad story: that of an unfaithful wife murdered by her husband.

"Miss Gee" may derive part of its appeal from being the only known ballad on cancer; the distinction of "Victor" comes solely from the way in which Auden's ironical humor, psychological relevance, and pathos transform the ordinary tale. Auden's skill at succinct narration is also demonstrated, for in thirty-seven stanzas he tells of Victor's childhood, growth, work, his meeting with Anna, their courtship and marriage, her unfaithfulness and murder, his apprehension and ultimate reaction. In two stanzas,

> Victor and his father went riding
>   Out in a little dog-cart;
> His father took a Bible from his pocket and read,
>   "Blessed are the pure in heart."
>
> It was a frosty December,
>   It wasn't the season for fruits;
> His father fell dead of heart disease
>   While lacing up his boots,

he compresses much and brilliantly makes his point—or points—about Victor's strict fundamentalist upbringing and its ironies. Editor of *The Faber Book of Aphorisms*, and writer of many "shorts," Auden is obviously interested and accomplished in compression.

Auden's humor is frequently ironic, as in the above stanzas, and depends on brevity and immediately confuting juxtaposition. In the stanza,

> He stood there above the body,
>   He stood there holding the knife;
> And the blood ran down the stairs and sang;
>   "I'm the Resurrection and the Life,"

the conjunction of "knife" and "Life," especially where "Life" is the essence of existence as God, is humorous, for it fulfills one of the essential characteristics of the comic which is conflict. In this instance the comedy, regardless of its near blas-

[21]

phemy and involvement with the bloody details of the murder, helps to diminish some of Victor's guilt—first, because it distances us somewhat from the terror of the act, and second, because its substance recalls to us the evangelical conditioning of Victor's childhood. His hearing God's voice approving his action to punish the sinner tempers the nature of his crime to the extent that we realize that it is his father's voice he has heard. Again, as in "Miss Gee," the comic dimension qualifies and moderates the tragic.

"O What is that Sound which so Thrills the Ear" may be Auden's best-known and most widely anthologized ballad, perhaps because with nine stanzas it is considerably shorter than "Miss Gee" or "Victor." Although its stanza form,

> O what is that sound which so thrills the ear
> Down in the valley drumming, drumming?
> Only the scarlet soldiers, dear,
> The soldiers coming,

is not that of the traditional ballad, its narrative presentation, rhyme, repetition, and musical insistence suggest that it is a ballad altered by Auden's interest in metrical innovation and variety. The poem—essentially more serious than either "Miss Gee" or "Victor"—is important to discuss because it demonstrates even more clearly than those ballads how subtle and flexible Auden's comic mode can be.

Auden accomplishes a remarkable feat in this poem by developing the terror of the invading soldiers at the same time that several ironies impart a vein of comedy to the speakers, a husband who answers his wife's questions about the approaching force of redcoats. From the outset there is a basis for irony in "thrills," for by the end of the poem the sound chills. There is the growing apprehension of the interrogating wife,

> O what are they doing with all that gear,
> What are they doing this morning, this morning?

[22]

and (until the penultimate stanza) the continuing complacency of the husband,

> Only the usual manoeuvres, dear,
> Or perhaps a warning.

Moreover, with further irony it is clear that to the husband the "warning" is not for them or really to be taken. The wife's fearful insistence,

> O is it the parson they want, with white hair,
> Is it the parson, is it, is it?

adds to the developing sinister atmosphere and also sets up the wry comedy of the husband's reply:

> No, they are passing his gateway, dear,
> Without a visit.

The rhymed stress on "visit" consummately marks the incongruity of the normal custom and the soldier's world.

Finally, the sudden abandonment of the wife by the husband and his selfish, specious reasoning,

> No, I promised to love you, dear,
> But I must be leaving,

is another comic element in the midst of terror. The concluding stanza, spoken by the wife—now abandoned by her husband —records her compelling fear as the soldiers'

> . . . boots are heavy on the floor
> And their eyes are burning.

Without diminishing the terror Auden dramatizes through comedy how ignorance of the military and abandonment of personal vows of love are part of the world in which force breaks the lock and splinters the door. The deft audacity with which Auden does this contributes to the unique satisfaction which this and other light works of Auden's give.

Another form which Auden uses for his light verse is the very brief poem. In his latest collected edition he includes

[23]

selections of epigrams under the general title "Shorts"; in the more recent *About the House* he calls a section of these poems "Symmetries and Asymmetries." "Asymmetries" are poems without rhyme resembling haiku; "Symmetries" are single couplets. All these brief pieces in whatever style and from whatever period are deftly illuminating: some ironic,

> The friends of the born nurse
> Are always getting worse

some with more direct humor,

> I'm afraid there's many a spectacled sod
> Prefers the British Museum to God

some with ratiocinative agility,

> Those who will not reason
> Perish in the act;
> Those who will not act
> Perish for that reason.

Auden's haiku (he became interested in the form while translating those of Dag Hammarskjöld) are more subtle than his rhymed "Symmetries," but all his "shorts," the new no less than the old, touch some part of the human condition that is far from inconsequential.

Like John Skelton, whose sixteenth-century metrics fascinated Auden so much that he has written many poems in them, Auden is never irrelevant in his lightness. In Skeltonics, a simple irregular tripping meter in short lines rhyming in two's and three's, Auden, like the earlier poet, is a poet using the unusual for a purpose. In an era of very serious poetry he adopts light verse frequently for satire and always for a rhetorical revitalization of the language. Auden, like Skelton, employs a kind of shock as therapy.

In his early poetry Auden used more or less exact Skeltonic lines which are brief and irregular as well as rhymed, as in "Too Dear, Too Vague" (1930):

[24]

> Love by ambition
> Of definition
> Suffers partition
> And cannot go
> From yes to no,
> For no is not love; no is no.

In this poem satirical of love's fickleness the nature of the lines fits the theme. Moreover, Auden here, as in most of his Skeltonic poems, breaks the traditional pattern down even further by departing from the expected and exact rhyme:

> Assured of all,
> The sofas creak,
> And were this all, love were
> But cheek to cheek
> And dear to dear.

The practice here is especially effective because it underlines the theme of the irresolution of a love which "would not gather another to another."

Auden still uses a kind of Skeltonic stanza, but seldom with the rhymed emphasis of his earlier versions. In "The Geography of the House," for example, the opening stanza is typical of his recent usage:

> Seated after breakfast
> In this white-tiled cabin
> Arabs call *the House where*
> *Everybody goes,*
> Even melancholics
> Raise a cheer for Mrs.
> Nature for the primal
> Pleasures she bestows.

But his abandonment of the more exuberantly rhymed Skeltonics (and the ballad) does not mean that Auden has become less interested in light verse than formerly. In fact, since 1940 he has written more comic and humorous pieces than in his early period, but, of course, that period by definition lasts only twelve years, from 1928 to 1940. Some of his finest comic poems—"Under Which Lyre" (1947), "The Love Feast" (1951), and "On the Circuit" (1965)—are late ones.

One of Auden's most delightful light poems is the song "Some Say That Love's a Little Boy" (1940), which dramatically demonstrates Auden's dissatisfaction with the ordinary. In alternating stanzas the poem presents commonplace views,

> Some say that love's a little boy,
> And some say it's a bird,

followed by questions in Auden's own eccentric idiom:

> Does it look like a pair of pyjamas
> Or the ham in a temperance hotel?
> Does its odor remind one of llamas,
> Or has it a comforting smell?

To Auden the truth about love or anything, in serious or light verse, must have the stamp of uniqueness on it or it will not satisfy him. This is why he is so attached to the comic mode; essentially he defines the comic situation as the individual in conflict with the traditional. And about the predicament of the individual Auden is very serious: in his critical analysis of the modern romantic temper in *The Enchafèd Flood* (1950) he uses Lewis Carroll's *The Hunting of the Snark* for significant exposition as well as *Moby Dick*.

Forty years after the appearance of his first poetry in 1928 Auden, reviewing his career, published a poem presenting himself as Autolycus (the rogue from *The Winter's Tale*). The choice of character is typical of Auden, for not only is it eccentric, it is also, paradoxically, self-effacing. In "Forty Years On" he admits that today's "audience would bar my ballads: it calls for Songs of Protest," and in envisioning

> the mouth of a cave by which (I know in my dream) I am
> to make my final exit
> its roof so low it will need an awkward duck to make it

[26]

he appears to conjure up the possibility of an ignominious end or loss of reputation. But Autolycus-Auden asks, "Well, will that be so shaming?" and quickly answers, "Why should it be? When has Autolycus ever solemned himself?"

Neither early nor late in his career has Auden ever solemned himself as person or poet. In his "Letter to Lord Byron" he qualifies both poetry and poets: ". . . novel writing is/ A higher art than poetry . . . / The average poet by comparison/ Is unobservant, immature, and lazy." In 1963 Auden was still applying strictures on the poet. "Poets are," he writes in "The Poet and the City," "by the nature of their interests and the nature of artistic fabrication, singularly ill-equipped to understand politics or economics." Auden's reasons for disqualifying poets from politics do not depreciate the poet as poet: "Their natural interest is in singular individuals and personal relations, while politics and economics are concerned with large numbers of people, hence with the human average (the poet is bored to death by the idea of The Common Man)." Following his objective analysis Auden states: "Society has always to beware of the utopias being planned by artists manqués over cafeteria tables late at night." A true poet would be content to deal with individuals, a common man, perhaps, but not The Common Man. Auden strives to be such a poet.

Auden is distressed by poets who lack modesty and honesty, the "self-proclaimed," who, as he described them in "Ode to Terminus" (1968), in order to "wow an audience, utter some resonant lie." Auden discusses the role and limit of poetry in *Secondary Worlds* (four lectures of 1967) and states what has always been apparent in his work, that there are two realms which we know: the primary or real world of the phenomena we experience through our senses and the secondary world of the arts. Of the two genres the primary one is of more importance. For example, he writes that "Social Justice is more important than the cause of art." Moreover, Auden emphasizes that it is a fatal delusion to believe that "by making works of art, we can do anything to eradicate [gross evils] or alleviate [appalling misery]." Auden, in brief, thinks that the concept of the *engagé* artist is untenable, that "the political and social history of Europe would be what it has been if Dante, Goethe, Titian, Mozart, Beethoven, *et al.* had never existed." Yet Auden is not so devastatingly restrictive on art's influence and role as this statement might first indicate. For he adds that, if he believes that art cannot be "effective as serious action," he does not mean it should be "frivolous action." And he maintains that "to believe in the value of art is to believe that it is possible to make an object, be it epic or a two-line epigram, which will remain permanently on hand in the world." This function of art, Auden points out, is quite different from much of the world's work, which is to make things that are designed to become obsolete. One definite "action" connected with the work of art that is "effective," therefore, is to teach us that "social and technological change are not as fatal to a genuine work of art as we are inclined to fear." The work of art can thus be engaged in giving us needed moral and intellectual sustenance. Auden puts this position even more impressively in his poem "In Memory of W. B. Yeats" (1939), where he first states rather deflatingly that "poetry makes nothing happen," but then qualifies this statement at the conclusion of the poem by invoking the poet to "persuade us to rejoice" and to "teach the free man how to praise." Clearly, Auden's aims for art are modest. Rather than make things "happen," which implies direct significant action, art is involved with more subtle actions: persuading and teaching. Its sphere of action is within the individual, not the political world.

"Moon Landing," an ode of 1969, clearly shows the kind of

engagement that Auden has with society. As the title and subject of this poem indicate, he does not ignore the world contemporary to him—although at the same time he typically uses the alcaic meter of the classical past.

From the opening lines,

> It's natural the Boys should whoop it up for
> so huge a phallic triumph,

which wittily reveal his use of Freudian psychology, Auden denounces the achievement of the moon landing as one that destroys our reverence for the moon and its awesome reign as "Queen of the Heavens." Always a champion of privacy, he also observes that

> Homer's heroes were no braver than Armstrong,
> Aldrin, Collins, but more fortunate: Hector
>   was excused the insult of having
>   his valor covered by television.

But more particularly he laments the new *hybris* of the technocrat, and, borrowing a Russian word undoubtedly learned through his interest in Voznesensky, he warns that

> Our apparatniks will continue making
> the usual squalid mess called History.

In conclusion, Auden significantly supports and defines the artist's special role in society:

> all we can pray for is that artists,
> chefs and saints may still appear to blithe it

in spite of "History." The poet who in 1935 asked his reader to discover "the leaping light for your delight" ("On This Island"), who in 1939 invoked the poet "to persuade us to rejoice" ("In Memory of W. B. Yeats"), and who beseeches the artist in 1969 to "blithe" our world is indeed a poet who knows that poetry has a purpose, one consistently involved more with personal than political or historical fulfillment.

Because Auden believes that art does have a practical limit to its engagement with the primary world, but that it does have nonetheless a permanent and valuable role to play, he hopes that "it is possible that artists may become both more modest and self-assured, that they may develop both a sense of humor about their vocation and a respect for that most admirable of Roman deities, the god Terminus." Auden, in fact, from his earliest work has been this kind of poet, never doctrinaire or didactic. Early, as mentioned above, lampooning Marx; late, as Autolycus, overtly satirizing himself, and, in "Ode to Terminus," denouncing the "colossal immodesty" of our whole society.

Auden's sense of humility is an important factor in his poetry, because not only does it contribute to his work its characteristic moderation, but it also is responsible for his concern for the individual. It is difficult, of course, to assess priority here. Since humility is rarely learned and is an aspect of personality, it may be truer to hold it to be the first cause. It could also be, however, that an interest in the individual and an understanding of small accomplishments, rather than, say, the economic aspirations of a class or state, enable Auden himself to be "modest" as well as "self-assured."

One of Auden's most impressive early poems, "Which Side Am I Supposed to Be On?" (now "Ode"), brilliantly shows the disposition of Auden to analyze honestly and to discover within ourselves the source of evil in society. The poem well represents Auden as a poet who deals with existence in terms of the individual rather than in terms of an ideology or system.

The ode opens in a typical Auden setting, a situation of anonymous crisis, one side ranked against the other. Here, involved with a group, we are "aware of our rank and alert to obey orders." All at the front, including "the youngest drummer," are "perfectly certain" about the myths of the nation for

[30]

which they are fighting. It is significant, however, that Auden makes it clear that this certainty comes not "from the records" nor from "the unshaven agent" who, returning dying to camp, "collapsed at our feet." Auden himself seeks to assess reality honestly by giving a retrospective history of a "recruit" which establishes the "quarrel" and the "aggressor" to be within himself and his, our own, world:

> At five you sprang, already a tiger in the garden.

The anonymity of Auden's scenes of action and crisis is important to this and other poems, for it dramatically reinforces the point of these poems, that our drama takes place, not in a recognized locale, but in a region really unknown to us, within ourselves.

"Our" forces as well as those of the enemy in "Ode" are shown to be remarkably similar. "We" parade in front of the Cathedral, are blessed by the Bishop, and indict the enemy who "fought against God." But "at the same hour" the "oppressors" shout,

> We will fight till we lie down beside
> The Lord we have loved.

Auden identifies in the camp of the alleged enemy our real enemies: Fear, Wrath, Envy, Gluttony, Greed, Acedia, and Lust. These, of course, are the traditional seven capital or deadly sins—with the exception of Fear which in this list takes the place of Pride, perhaps to make the perceptive analysis that Pride originates in Fear. Lust, with memorable Freudian wit, is described as

> That skillful sapper,
> Muttering to his fuses in a tunnel "Could I meet here with
> Love, I would hug her to death."

The atmosphere in this justly famous poem is of war and opposition, the opening is of "watching with binoculars" the distant

[31]

lines, and Auden describes these figures as those for whom "for a very long time/ We've been on the look-out." But he reminds us, "some of them, surely, we seem to have seen before." Not, however, through the binoculars trained on the enemy's camp, but in our own lives: "that girl," for example, "who rode off on her bicycle one fine summer evening/ And never returned." The poem ends, as it began, with the mood of heightened tension:

> All leave is cancelled; we must say good-bye,
> We entrain at once for the North; we shall see in the morning
> The headlands we're doomed to attack.

Its concluding line, "We shall lie out there," is one of power, for "lie" is a pun on the untruth in not recognizing the internal and private nature of the warfare. The "headlands we're doomed to attack," in this poem, are cerebral rather than geographical.

The answer to the question "Which side am I supposed to be on?" is clearly "on the side of the individual," for Auden unquestionably establishes the individual as the source of any society's character, and such a belief confers special value to what, in a system, might appear small and ordinary. He naturally, therefore, in "Who's Who" (1933) relates with undisguised pleasure the situation where the simple person influences the great. When in 1940 he wrote "The Unknown Citizen" to protest the totalitarian manipulation of the little person, the theme, although greatly prophetic of the ensuing years, had long been Auden's.

In no poem since 1939 has Auden indicated any change from his celebration of the individual. "The Old Man's Road" (1956) presents Auden's allegiance to what in a poem he describes as that which has "lost purpose," namely, the individual pursuit of one's "true self." The protagonist of the poem proceeds "through our whole landscape"

[32]

Ignoring God's vicar and God's Ape,

as if such a path "were still in vogue." "True to His where-
fore," the Old Man's Road "threads its odd way," and in
Auden's context "His" refers to both the Old Man and God.
Auden's God is He who confers dignity and freedom on his
creatures. No one "can be made captive" who follows this
way of the individualist. In this position, remarkably similar
to that of Auden at Oxford (as described by Spender), he
praises those

> Who never ask what History is up to,
> So cannot act as if they knew:
> Assuming a freedom its Powers deny,
> Denying its Powers, they pass freely.

To "pass freely" might be taken as Auden's motto. In his crisis
landscape of the early poetry, danger is described as closed
borders, revocation of passports, and the ambush. As seen
especially in *The Quest*, his compelling sonnet sequence of
twenty poems (1941), a Kierkegaardian imperative for search
and becoming is an important concern of Auden's. His love of
travel and residence in many countries—England, Iceland,
China, Italy, Germany, Austria, the United States—may with
reason be related to this necessity. To be "without hindrance"
is as vital to him today as it was in 1956 or 1939 or 1928, for
he recently disclosed that when he learned that Congress was
considering the double taxation of citizens who lived abroad,
he intended to give up his U.S. citizenship in favor of an Ice-
landic one. There is no doubt where Auden's first allegiance
lies. Selfish, perhaps, but it is a position which gives selves to
all and which substitutes the aspiration to "pass freely" for the
more selfishly aggrandizing slogan, "they shall not pass."

Auden knows, moreover, that to pursue one's "true self" is
not, in the depreciative sense, to be selfish. His translation of
Voznesensky's "Parabolic Ballad," which he includes in *About*

[33]

the House, clearly depicts the hazards of departing from the usual. "The parabola doesn't come to us easily," he writes; it takes courage to follow one's own bent: Voznesensky's protagonist ends up in Siberia. Auden's praise of this poet and his particular interest in this poem are indeed consistent with his own work. Even more to the point of defending Auden from the charge of self-serving selfishness in his championing of individualism is his refusal to sanction isolation from one's fellow men.

Auden continually uses islands to symbolize refuges that beckon to man, but he categorically rejects such a choice, however alluring it may be. His "Paysage Moralisé" (1933), a seminal poem in Auden's canon, the title of which names Auden's special skill of giving landscapes appropriate meanings, concludes with the wish that "we rebuild our cities, not dream of islands." In Auden's appreciative metaphorical landscape no one becomes an island: Edward Lear, for example, becomes "a land," and Yeats possesses "provinces," "squares," and "suburbs." Nor does his long dramatic poem *The Sea and the Mirror*, which portrays the mutual needs of Prospero and Caliban, a theme which honors all reality, support the symbolic isolation of islands.

Auden's recognition of Caliban as well as Prospero, the primary world as well as the secondary, illustrates an important facet of his recognition of the individual—his informing humility. Not merely a question of minimizing his own achievements or of accepting the common man, it is a positive commitment to all the reality of what he calls the "primary world." No aloof aesthete, Auden recognizes that the world in which he lives, like himself, is far from perfect.

"Nones," a long ode of 1948 which is one of a series called "Horae Canonicae," further illustrates Auden's view of the world. Although it is not all sweetness and light, there is no

[34]

retreat to islands or regret that such a removal is not to be made. The human situation described resembles somewhat that of *The Waste Land*. There is a feeling of ominous malaise:

> The day is too hot, too bright, too nothing,
> Too ever, the dead remains too nothing,
> What shall we do till nightfall?

This is a world which is to be "Blown up, buried down, cracked open"; the time when "The hangman has gone to wash, the soldiers to eat" and "We are left alone with our feat." We are constantly faced with "this death." Yet in confronting this burden, Auden in the concluding two stanzas states his consoling outlook which justifies the calm and elevated tone of the whole poem. His hope is in the individual, as we have come to expect; no system of any kind is sought. Auden's consolatory plea is for the individual to "go home," return, that is, to himself, and that, resting, "our own wronged flesh"

> May work undisturbed, restoring
> The order we try to destroy.

Auden, in his final imagery from the natural world, suggests confidence that man can also find his place in this world. And although he shall be "awed by death" in a world where the hawk looks down on "smug hens" in "their pecking order" and the bug has a "view balked by grass," yet—in his final line —there are symbolic deer who "Peer through chinks in the forest."

As at the outset of his career when (in "The Letter") he expressed the will to be "decent with the seasons," Auden still seeks a harmony analogous to that statement rather than a mindless surrender to Nature. Nature gives him metaphors of order, a paradigm which assigns meaning to the individual, but Man must also be apart from the natural world in many ways. "Taller Today," an early poem of lyrical resolution (formerly titled "As Well As Can Be Expected"), shows Auden's inter-

[35]

pretation of Nature. He opens with pastoral scenes to represent the love expressed, but ultimately the human feeling is distinguished from anything in Nature:

> Noises at dawn will bring
> Freedom for some, but not this peace
> No bird can contradict.

It is the human quality of loving and enduring which Auden celebrates, and man's special peace here comes from knowing that man can love in spite of Nature's glacier which he can endure. Auden in his honest humility glosses over nothing in the nature of man or the physical world. The consoling use that Auden makes of the physical world is ultimately to illustrate man's uniqueness within it, however instructive and metaphorically effective his relationship to it may be. Although Auden ends "Nones" with a natural scene evocative of a measure of hope, its relevance is to men within a different (although analogous) order. "Belial," we learn earlier in the poem, waits to "make our wives waltz naked." Although man is "like all the creatures now watching this spot," the "like" introduces a simile and not an equivalence. The "order" that Auden in this poem urges us to restore is analogous to that of Nature, but specifically it is man's nature which Auden is talking about. Auden is not a poet of Nature; as in "Nones," he uses analogies from Nature to support his plea for man to put aside anxiety and accept his own nature or self.

"A Change of Air" (1963) is, to use Auden's word, a "parable" to illustrate this continuing theme. Regardless of how much we hanker after the "flashy errands of our dreams" he warns that "To go Elsewhere is to withdraw from movement," where "Elsewhere" is the region outside of one's self. "Your sojourn there," Auden warns, "will remain a wordless/ Hiatus in your voluble biography." Significantly in style and

[36]

theme Auden sponsors the selfhood which honestly compre-
hends even its "Corns, heartburn," and "sinus headaches." There
is no Elsewhere or island refuge for the honest mind. To "pass
freely" in the way of a meaningful life Auden cultivates the
self's truth. The hero of a modern poem, he writes, should be

neither the "Great Man" nor the romantic rebel, both doers of
extraordinary deeds, but the man or woman in any walk of life
who despite all the impersonal pressures of modern society, man-
ages to acquire and preserve a face of his own.

One of Auden's loveliest lyrics, "On This Island" (1933),
a poem that creates a mood of contemplative vision, gives what
may be the essential purpose of all of Auden's work: that
"the full view/ Indeed may enter." The "full view" that Auden
describes here is a distant vista of ships which, although on
"urgent" errands, from the distance of "the chalk wall" appear
to "saunter" through the summer water as gently as the clouds.
The observer is urged to "stand stable" and "silent be" to hear
"the swaying sound of the sea," and to "pause" while "the
shingle scrambles after the sucking surf." The emphasis on
"now" in the opening line ("Look stranger, on this island
now") makes the whole poem part of a larger paradox, that for
England in the midst of the Great Depression Auden should
advance such a gentle direction as "stand stable." Surely the
"now" demanded exploitation of elements like "urgent," "sucking surf," and "knock of the tide." But such a poem would
not be Auden's. His interpretation of a poem is that it "is
beautiful or ugly to the degree that it succeeds or fails in
reconciling contradictory feelings in an order of mutual pro-
priety." Although Auden wrote this definition long after the
poem "On This Island," he has also told us that his views on
poetry have never changed. And the attitude and tone of
reasonable balance of early poems like "The Letter" and "Taller

[37]

Today" confirm the example of "On This Island" as a demonstration of this central characteristic of Auden's poetry.

Anthologists have rightly claimed "Musée des Beaux Arts" as one of their favorite pieces of Auden's, for its description of the vision of the Old Masters embodies Auden's own concepts of poetry as a reconciliation of the various and the contradictory. "How well they understood," he writes, how suffering takes place "While someone else is eating or opening a window" or how

> . . . when the aged are reverently, passionately waiting
> For the miraculous birth, there always must be
> Children who did not specially want it to happen, skating
> On a pond at the edge of a wood.

Auden perceives that in a corner of a "dreadful martyrdom"

> . . . the dogs go on with their doggy life and the
>   torturer's horse
> Scratches its innocent behind on a tree.

It is Brueghel's *Icarus*, however, that Auden particularly describes: how the disappearing white legs are casually ignored or unnoticed by all in the scene. Auden does not indicate approval of each case of indifference; that the "expensive delicate ship . . . Had somewhere to get to and sailed calmly on" clearly conveys a tone of critical irony. But to Brueghel—as well as to Auden—such is the composition of reality. Much of Auden's technique—his irony and his use of the odd, for example—is the embodiment or portrait of the dichotomous and opposing variety which fills his own perspective.

Auden's "full view" results in a tempered tone (to use the musical sense of "temper" as "adjust to harmony") which, judging from "The Horatians" (a poem of 1969 that describes temperaments like his), also appears to be Horatian. The term is useful to apply to Auden, not only because it originates from his own work, but also because of its association with satire.

[38]

And the very concept of mild, that is, Horatian, satire in itself reconciles contradictory aspects. Auden is and always has been a moderate poet—where "moderate" is a position between extremes. Auden's early long dramatic poem, *Paid on Both Sides*, effectively illustrates the Auden of this temperament. The setting is stark with no scenery (according to the poet's directions). The two hostile parties of Lintzgarth and Nattrass are distinguished by different colored arm bands, and as in "Which Side Am I Supposed to Be On?" it is difficult to identify one adversary from the other. As is usual in Auden's crisis landscapes, the scene is of internecine warfare of indeterminate cause with the action more symbolic of moral conditions than political. There is also a chorus which complements with classical rigor the elliptical quality of the verse.

Auden is possessed by the thought that it is difficult, if not at times impossible, to know which is the "right" side. So here in *Paid* there is little to choose between the Nowers of Lintzgarth and the Shaws of Nattrass. In fact, it seems that Auden solicits the rejection of both these parties as representatives of an older Europe, for in a brief scene one of the Nowers leaves for the Colonies with the statement, "I feel I must get away from here. There is not enough room." Yet this rejection is made with immediate qualification: the emigrant realizes that "the actual moving is unpleasant." And more will appear later.

The dramatic poem is full of watchers, spies, and ambushes, endless retaliation by one "side" against the other. In conclusion, however, John Nower and Anne Shaw announce their engagement and momentarily the warfare ceases; George Nower and Seth Shaw shake hands. But the peace does not even last through the day of celebration: Seth's mother urges him to kill John Nower to revenge the death of Seth's brother. The concluding speeches of Anne and the Chorus emphasize the fleeting nature of happiness, the cyclical aspect of doom and joy which is "now not." The dour chorus intones that man "is defeated." But its final speech marks that although man must "give up his breath, his woman" and that there will be "no life to touch," there will later on be "Big fruit, eagles above the stream." The injustice of this ironical situation is part of Auden's attitude, and it supports that brief but important scene where one man departs from his society. "Now not" is Auden's target (the departure is made by a Now-er); "Big fruit" later offers little solace. *Paid on Both Sides* is indisputably a poem of protest, but it is informed by restraint. There is consolation as well as distress in knowing that "both sides" get "paid," that "no man is strong." There may be a solution in departure, but in the complexity of Auden's "full view" the poem implies that departure will be no simple panacea. Clearly it must not lead to the creation of another "side" (if only of one) of hostile division.

Borders, divisions, and limits to personal freedom are central concerns of the three plays which Auden wrote in the middle thirties with Christopher Isherwood. The Lintzgarth-Nattrass rivalry of *Paid on Both Sides* is enlarged to nationalistic proportions in the rivalries between Ostnia and Westland in *The Dog Beneath the Skin* (1935) and *On the Frontier* (1938); and in *The Ascent of F6* (1936) Ostnia is the name given to the nation competing with Britain for colonial power.

Of the plays, the first, *The Dog Beneath the Skin*, is the most poetic and lively, as its cryptic and whimsical title might suggest. Although the play ends with a Marxist tag, "To each his need: from each his power," the piece is not about politics or economics but the needs and powers of human love. The protagonist masquerading as a dog to learn the truth about men finds them less than human in their hatred. Condign punishment in the end turns them into appropriate animals: the ultimate irony is that the dog is not beneath the skin but all too

[40]

obvious. The work's subtitle, "Where Is Francis?," is the key to the theme, the need to find one's human self in the midst of various disabling divisions and tyrannies: in England, those of family, class, and depression; abroad, those of armed borders and oppressing monarchy and dictatorship (Ostnia-Westland).

Auden and Isherwood have given the subtitle "A Play" to *The Dog Beneath the Skin* and "A Tragedy" to *The Ascent of F6*. The terms are appropriate: certainly *Dog* is the most effervescent and playful; *F6* ends with the death of the protagonist, who loses his life because of a tragic flaw. At the outset of the work Michael Ransom, a skilled amateur mountain climber, is approached by his statesman brother with a plea to be the first to climb F6, a mountain between British Sudoland and Ostnian Sudoland, for the Ostnians had already begun to climb the peak to impress the natives and weaken British influence in the region. Ransom—dramatizing Auden's own views—refuses, realizing that he is being used to further the kind of jingoistic nationalism that he despises. Finally coaxed by his mother, Michael gives in, and against his own principles accomplishes the ascent, bringing victory to Britain, honor to his brother, satisfaction to his mother, and death to himself and his companions. Ransom is well named: he is indeed the price paid for deliverance—of others. His tragic death, as the final chorus states, has "made Man's weakness known," and we learn, not as in a traditional tragedy that immutable external laws cannot be transgressed, but that personal values cannot be abandoned without psychological death.

John Fuller has perceptively remarked that the third play, *On the Frontier*, is close to the medium of opera. Called a "melodrama" by its authors, it is the least subtle of the three, and many readers will not agree with Francis Scarfe that it is Auden's best.

The theme of *Frontier* is similar to that of the earlier plays and its situation is very much like that of *Paid on Both Sides* except that it offers a more explicit solution. The scene is of nationalistic hatred and warfare: real frontiers which prevent men from passing freely amongst each other and fulfilling themselves. As in *Paid*, two lovers defy the division, but in *Frontier*, amidst a perverse East-West war, they die united resolutely in love. The comments of the dying lovers are significant because they embody the reasonable balance of Auden's mind. One of the lovers asks if the world will ever have a place for those like them. The other's answer is that although this is a "world of faults and suffering and death" one cannot "stand apart." His concluding statement is to propose

> To build the city where
> The will to love is done.

The departure or quest for a life of the fulfilled self is not to seek easy and isolated refuge. The frontier, wherever and whatever it is, is a baneful symbol to Auden. "To build the city" (not to seek islands) is his metaphor for the mature act of the individual who in rejecting the world of "sides" strives for reconciliation of individuals—not by removing differences but by honoring them. It is for Auden a moderating and tempering act.

Moderation is also the theme of "In Praise of Limestone" (1948), one of Auden's best-known poems. Even his recent revision (he does not exclusively edit early works) in which he excises "dildo" (slang for penis) indicates that temperament of his. He does seek surprise and his poetry is characterized by the unusual, but the effect is always, as he tells us he wants it to be, qualified by the "drab sober" and in balance. Although he has not commented on his deletion of "dildo," there is a reasonable explanation: without it, nearby in the poem there is enough shock in the description of the ideal god who should

[42]

be pacified by a "clever line or a good lay." The "full view" is not unbalanced or extreme.

Auden's point in "Limestone" is that moderation is most desirable. Permanence is not always really welcome: "Sins can be forgiven" and "bodies rise from the dead." Statues—"modifications of matter"—enhance our pleasure and their material. What is unyielding as marble reminds him of death and makes him "uneasy"; what is too yielding like water makes him sad, for it speaks to him only of solitude and the absence of love. He rejects both as "immoderate" and eulogizes the limestone landscape of England which to a reasonable degree is both permanent and possible to modify. Auden's most important metaphor of "paysage moralisé" is that of limestone.

> When I try to imagine a faultless love,
>   Or the life to come,

he concludes, "what I see is/ a limestone landscape." How apt this metaphor is to describe Auden is seen by his rejection of both marble and water for being too predictable, a quality associated with extremes. Auden's praising limestone because it is an easily modified material is entirely reasonable: the true moderate chooses not what is obdurate but what can be moderated or changed.

Auden has had an even longer fascination with the city as a metaphor for the environment which he posits as good for man. "To build the city" was the closing plea of *On the Frontier*, and in "City Without Walls" thirty-one years later he still reveals his commitment. The new poem, moreover, in its dramatic presentment of three voices without direct comment from the poet still shows the interest that led him to write three plays with Isherwood. Auden has worked frequently in collaboration (also with MacNeice and Chester Kallman), perhaps because it is in itself a dramatic and moderating activity.

[43]

In Auden's setting for "City Without Walls" there are two apartments contiguous to his, each of which contributes an important dimension to the work. Most of the poem presents the first speaker's views of the city as he lies awake tossing in troubled thought at 3 A.M. He is particularly disturbed by the many terrors of the city, the "Asphalt Land," where "after dark" one is reckless to walk "in that wilderness." "All," he laments, "has gone phut."

But these black musings are suddenly interrupted by a voice from the next apartment:

> "What fun and games you find it to play
> Jeremiah-cum-Juvenal."

And it is interesting to observe that the speaker's reference is to Juvenal, for when he continues in complaint and chides the first speaker, " 'Shame on you for your Schadenfreude!,' " we begin to reflect that the long opening tirade is indeed bitter and a little morbid. The concluding lines, those of the third voice from another apartment, direct both previous speakers to " 'Go to sleep now for God's sake!' " with the added simple belief that " 'You both will feel better by breakfast time.' "

These voices in dramatic conjunction establish in context a dominant tone and attitude. For one thing, the long opening section of Juvenalian rejection gives credibility to the first interruption. The rebuff is justified. The third voice, which is described as "bored," utters what we must accept as inadequate platitudes; it cannot be accepted as Auden's view, for it is simplistic and too yielding in abject acceptance. Nor can the opening view of equally extreme bitterness be credited to Auden. The second speaker who reproves one extremist and who in turn is denounced by another, who is, therefore, the man in the middle (neither marble nor water), seems closer to what we find compatible with Auden's "limestone" views. The poem dramatically portrays the unreasonableness of both the extreme

[44]

pessimist and the extreme optimist and commends the milder, middle perspective. The rejection of Juvenal suggests an alternative.

In "The Horatians" Auden appreciatively addresses Horace and his followers as "you." But at the conclusion of the ode he quotes one of Horace's descendants who uses "we." The transition from the second person to the first has the effect—despite the quotation marks—of suggesting that Auden himself is speaking as one of the Horatians. The rhetorical effect also tends to enlist the reader as a Horatian.

There is indeed, on the basis of this poem's description of what is Horatian, almost no basis to exclude Auden from this category. The opening lines inform Horace himself that he could not be imagined in the "Courts of Grand Opera," although we know Auden's interest in the opera as a genre and as a writer of several libretti (*The Rake's Progress* with music by Stravinsky may be the best known). Auden, in *The Dyer's Hand*, a collection of essays (1963), has praised the world of opera as "the last refuge of the High Style." This qualification, however, is one that fits Auden's theory of combining the eccentric with the traditional. He demands originality, the anomalous in the midst of the sober. If he were a Horatian, he would have to be a unique one— one that might, for instance, love the opera.

In "The Horatians" Auden attributes to Horatians "knowledge of local topography," a classification which readily calls to mind Auden's praise of a limestone landscape and his wide use of appreciative metaphors of landscape. "Your tastes," he tells the Horatians, "run to small dinner parties" and "the tone of voice that suits them." In *Secondary Worlds* Auden says that the modern poet "must speak in a quiet voice," and in his poem on dining, "Tonight at Seven-thirty" (*About the House*), he tells us that "the gathering should be small and unpublic."

[45]

Among the British branch of the Horatian family Auden writes that many "have found in the Anglican Church" an agreeable life. Auden also considers himself an Anglo-Catholic and an adherent to the tenets of that Church which has been called what indeed seems to be of Horatian aspect, a *via media*. Horatians, as Auden describes them, "never shoot . . . lovers," a disposition that matches the tender, forgiving attitude of Auden's "Lullaby" (never revised or rejected). His concluding remarks (in the first person of a Horatian) are "We can only"

> . . . look at
> this world with a happy eye,
> but from a sober perspective.

The paradox "happy"-"sober" conjures up the author himself who speaks of his happiness as well as his search for the unique within the "drab sober." Auden in this poem also observes to Horace that "enthusiastic/ Youth write you off as cold, who cannot be found on/ barricades," and one feels instinctively that Auden is modestly acknowledging his own lack of appeal to militants who would rather have him be the doctrinaire activist he never has been.

Auden's salient characteristic, then, the one that explains his important qualities of uniqueness and gaiety within the drab and sober, a continuing interest in privacy and the individual, and the preference for the comic, is a temperament disposed toward balance. Following his poem's description, this moderation might usefully be described further as Horatian.

Yet, in the final analysis, Auden resists rigid classification. His "full view" is too comprehensive to submit completely to the traditional term. Any poet deserves to be treated on his own terms, but none perhaps so much as Auden who has no peer in our time as a defender of the individual and whose work is nothing if not brilliantly unique.

[46]

SELECTED BIBLIOGRAPHY

·NOTE: *The works of Auden are published in the United States by Random House, in England by Faber and Faber.*

For the most useful and complete bibliography published to date, see B. C. Bloomfield (with a Foreword by Auden), W. H. Auden, a Bibliography: The Early Years through 1955, Charlottesville, 1964.

Principal Works of W. H. Auden

About the House. New York, 1965; London, 1966.
The Age of Anxiety. New York, 1947; London, 1948.
A Certain World. New York, 1970.
Chesterton. London, 1970.
City Without Walls. London, 1969; New York, 1970.
Collected Longer Poems. New York, 1967; London, 1968.
The Collected Poetry of W. H. Auden. New York, 1945.
Collected Shorter Poems, 1927–1957. London, 1966; New York, 1967.
The Dyer's Hand. New York, 1962; London, 1963.
Homage to Clio. New York, 1960; London, 1960.
Nones. New York, 1951; London, 1952.
On This Island. New York, 1937.
The Orators. London, 1932. Revised edition, New York, 1967; London, 1968.
The Oxford Book of Light Verse. London, 1938. (Edited with an Introduction by Auden.)
Poems. Oxford, 1928; London,ʼ1930; New York, 1934.
Secondary Worlds. New York, 1968; London, 1968.
The Shield of Achilles. New York, 1955; London, 1955.

Works Written with Christopher Isherwood

The Ascent of F6. London, 1936; New York, 1937.
The Dog Beneath the Skin. New York, 1935; London, 1935.
On the Frontier. New York, 1938; London, 1938.

Works Written with Louis MacNeice

Letters from Iceland. New York, 1937; London, 1937. Revised edition, London, 1967 (a paperback).

Critical Works and Commentary

Beach, Joseph Warren. The Making of the Auden Canon. Minneapolis, 1957.

Blair, J. G. The Poetic Art of W. H. Auden. Princeton, 1965.

Bloom, Robert. "The Humanization of Auden's Early Style," *PMLA*, LXXXIII (May, 1968), 443–54.

Brooks, Cleanth. "W. H. Auden as a Critic," *Kenyon Review*, XXVI (Winter, 1964), 173–89.

Callan, Edward. "The Development of W. H. Auden's Poetic Theory since 1940," *Twentieth-Century Literature*, IV (October, 1958), 79–91.

Cox, R. G. "The Poetry of W. H. Auden," in The Modern Age, Vol. VII of The Pelican Guide to English Literature, ed. Boris Ford. Baltimore, 1961.

Fuller, John. A Reader's Guide to W. H. Auden. London, 1970.

Greenberg, Herbert. Quest for the Necessary. Cambridge, Mass., 1968.

Grigson, Geoffrey, ed. *New Verse*, "Auden Double Number." November, 1937.

Hoggart, Richard. Auden: An Introductory Essay. London, 1951.

Isherwood, Christopher. Lions and Shadows. London, 1937; Norfolk, Conn., 1947.

Jarrell, Randall. "Changes of Attitude and Rhetoric in Auden's Poetry," *Southern Review*, VII (Autumn, 1941, 326–49.

—— "Freud to Paul: The Stages of Auden's Ideology," *Partisan Review*, XII (Fall, 1945), 437–57.

MacNeice, Louis. Modern Poetry: A Personal Essay. London, 1938.

Ostroff, Anthony, ed. "A Symposium on Auden's 'A Change of Air,'" with essays by George P. Elliott, Karl Shapiro, and Stephen Spender, and a reply by W. H. Auden, *Kenyon Review*, XXVI (Winter, 1964), 190–208.

Replogle, Justin. Auden's Poetry. Seattle and London, 1969.

Scarfe, Francis. Auden and After. London, 1942.

Spears, Monroe K., ed. Auden: A Collection of Critical Essays. Englewood Cliffs, 1964 (a paperback).

—— "The Dominant Symbols of Auden's Poetry," *Sewanee Review*, LIX (Summer, 1951), 392–425.

—— The Poetry of W. H. Auden: The Disenchanted Island. New York, 1963. Revised edition, New York, 1968 (a paperback).

Spender, Stephen. World Within World. London, 1951.